I0446810

HOW I GOT TO THE PERSON I NEEDED TO BE

A MONEY MEMOIR THAT COULD HELP YOU TOO

MICHELE WILLIAMS

Copyright © 2023 Inspiring Others Productions LLC

All rights reserved

No part of this publication may be used, reproduced, distributed, or transmitted in any form or by any means, electronic, mechanical, photocopying, scanning, recording, or otherwise, without the prior written permission of the publisher.

It must be noted that the author and publisher assume no responsibility or liability whatsoever on the behalf of the reader of this publication. The information provided in this publication is not intended to be legal or accounting advice. All readers are advised to seek competent lawyers and accountants to follow laws and regulations that may apply to specific situations.

ISBN: 9798872744023

Printed in the United States of America

"Every gold piece you save must work for you, every copper it earns, its child, must also earn for you. If you would become wealthy, then what you save must earn, and its children must earn."

– GEORGE S. CLASON, AUTHOR OF THE RICHEST MAN IN BABYLON

CONTENTS

To retired English Teacher Robin DuRant, a lovely friend and companion, who enjoys reading and has been a phenomenal source of help to me in putting together this book. I always looked forward to your feedback because they were always on point, ensuring I never left out any important formatting, affected demography, or particular topic. To you I say a special thank you.

To Cafeteria Worker Ivonne Medina, another good friend and companion, who enjoys social events and has been interested in my many ventures. I always loved how you showed such interest in what I did, whether I failed or succeeded. To you I say a special thank you for always being there.

FOREWORD

Ever thought of how you would divide the money if you won $600,000,000? Would you do quarter for emergency, quarter for retirement, quarter for backup, quarter for business; and remember, taxes and inflation do eat up your money too?

Emergencies, retirement, backup, and business are the four ways I divide my money to ensure I cover all the areas. Emergency money is useful for medical, bills, repairs, even death. Personal bank accounts, Roth IRAs, certificate of deposits, and automobiles are great assets for selling or withdrawing from to retrieve emergency money when needed. Additionally, giving to others reinforces what goes around comes around, so giving to various charities plays an important part as well. Work to put these emergency assets in place before age 18; preferably parents should guide and help start these assets for their kids then transfer later.

Retirement at age 30 is the goal for everyone. Social security, fixed annuities, trusts, pensions are designed to give you monthly income until you die using various techniques. Work to put these in place before your 30th birthday.

Backup money is always helpful when the worst happens like a natural disaster, a recession, business low periods. Put aside a lump sum amount of money to totally cover you, your family, your business during these low periods. Another way to do this is putting aside 25% profits as protection or putting aside 25% allowances for the unforeseeable.

But why should you listen to me? I'm giving you where you need to get to, a target. A target based on what I've learnt about money in my own life, and I'm sharing this with you. And maybe or maybe not I'm further ahead of the game than you, but here's what I've learnt over my 50+ years of existence. Here's how you too can get to the person you need to be. This book will show you.

Finally, everyone has a business idea, 90% of people just don't know they have one. Some people aren't even passionate enough about their own ideas. With any business, however, there will always be inherent risks. Business bank accounts, stocks, bonds, and properties are excellent income stream scenarios to set up and yield money. Other income stream scenarios are music and book and film royalties, restaurant income, information technology services income, TV network income, game show hosting income, online dating service income, laundry/dry cleaning services income, life insurance sales income, perfume sales income, fashion designs income, dance/strip club/escort services income, fitness/weight loss income, executive security services income, art museum income, hotel tourism income, stock exchange income and many more. Work to generate money from a business(es) before age 40.

So, when you're at age 40, when mid-life crisis occurs, you can look over your life and be satisfied rather than distressed about what you have set up for yourself and your family thus far.

HOW I GOT TO
THE PERSON
I NEEDED
TO BE

A MONEY MEMOIR THAT COULD
HELP YOU TOO

01 – EMERGENCY, RETIREMENT, BACKUP, BUSINESS

EMERGENCY

Now you might ask, what might this look like? Very different for each person, of course. Let's start with keeping a minimum of $30,000 in your personal bank account. Never go below that minimum.

Hang on, don't close the book yet, it's a target. I'm giving you where you need to get to. Starting from $0 and then working your way to maintaining $30,000 minimum in your bank account. REASON: There are so many things that can and may happen as you journey through life.

You want to give yourself an extra buffer, in the event the worst happens. Not to be caught unawares or, worse, unprepared. Again, these are targets I'm giving you based on what I've learnt about money in my own life.

Go ahead, open a Roth IRA the moment you turn age 18 or earlier and begin saving the maximum amount allowed on the 1st of every month. Why? You're paying yourself FIRST, why not! Open a certificate of deposit, saving even a bit more of your money. Keep expenses down for food, clothes, utilities, entertainment, rent, automobile(s). Rent should be no more than 20% of your after-tax income. Buy a reasonably priced automobile(s) and ensure to get comprehensive insurance (theft, liability, collision, medical payments, uninsured bodily injury, property damage); and please buy a good automobile so maintenance costs are low. Also, ensure to have life, medical, dental insurance. (If you have your own life insurance use it for savings too). And give, give tips, help a stranger, these are all part of building your emergency fund.

So, when an emergency comes up you can check your bank account, your Roth IRA (but be sure you're over 59 ½ years old before withdrawing or your one-time withdrawal is less than the amount you had put in), your certificate of deposit, your automobiles (if this is in good condition can run you a good sale price), your paintings (if you're a collector selling a piece in an emergency), your life insurance savings (just remember the amount withdrawn will be deducted from death benefits plus any accrued interest unless paid back), or even a stranger for the needed money.

RETIREMENT

Now retirement is a little tricky because it depends on how much money you know will be enough for you to live off when that time comes. And what time is that? Very different for each person, of course. Contribute to your social security. Open a fixed annuity that will pay you a monthly income until you die. Set up a trust(s) to protect your assets from creditors and probates (include lists of assets, wills, prenups). Contribute to your company's pension accounts to save the maximum amount allowed. But no matter how much you save, in this economic climate, even the right amount of social security, fixed annuities, trusts, pensions, would still be too small to fit the person you really need to be, the person you were born to be, the person you were put on the planet to become.

I told myself, towards the end of year 2017, after noticing my Curves gym I owned was going out of business, that I wanted to make $60 an hour, that's the minimum I would settle for. I got to that goal in 6 years, going back to doing what I loved, computers, as Systems Analyst II at the Los Angeles Department of Water and Power, after the gym closed. But what was interesting was that $60 an hour then was too small, I couldn't even max out the pension accounts the company offered. So, at the end of year 2023, I told myself I wanted to make 10,000 times the amount of money I made, that's the minimum I would settle for. I was already past age 30 swiftly running out of time.

I say that to say, you don't want to reach retirement and the amount you plan for ends up being too small. So, work it out. If I made $600,000 an hour, there's no way on earth and in heaven that amount would be too small to retire off. Now, it's time to get to work. How can I help people to be able to make this amount per hour? How can I add that kind of value to the marketplace? What can I do that I'm not doing? THINK, use your brain. Now, bear in mind this is my number not yours.

You will have your own retirement number. That's also good. Just multiply it by 4 or 10 or 12,000, because humans who are not yet aware of their spiritual greatness tend to set low goals for themselves.

So, now that I have a number, notice how I'm not adding up food expenses and automobile payments and mortgages to get to the total expenses in the future, then making sure the pension I would get covered it, No. What I'm doing is going the route that forces me to change myself into something or someone else who will get to this – what looks like an impossible goal.

Look inside yourself, what is that one thing you do when no one else is looking? You sing, sketch, doodle, masturbate, dance, jump, swim, do some weird things with your body or voice, you look like a freak, you're a genius, you do nothing? You suffered a stroke, you've lost all your limbs, you've had brain damage, you're a victim, you're homeless, you're powerless, you're a drug addict, you're a day dreamer? What is it that YOU do, that YOU can do, only YOU. It might be singing, drawing automobiles, break dancing, body painting, giving voice lessons, teaching others how to recover from a stroke, how to recover from brain damage, how to regain self-assertiveness, how to recover from fentanyl addiction. Your soul is going to follow that no matter what anybody says, that's just how it is. Your goal now is to continue following it, figure out how to offer your services to the public and make money doing it, and that is your retirement number right there.

Start making a list of what you're going to do – write, draw, sing, sell, design, create, gigolo, pornography, sex retreats, sew freaky outfits, play basketball, conduct training seminars, score touchdowns, swim marathons, cycle championships, draw inspiration from Jerry Seinfeld who created a TV series out of nothing if you can't yet figure out what you want to do, dance, act, play your saxophone/guitar/violin on the train and/or at the park (I'd love to hear more freelance musicians play on the train, whatever you have to do to generate profit from the public, legally, of course; and for God sake pay your taxes when the time comes), talk, read, film **(THE PLANT PHASE)**; keep selling what you do to the public for the next 6 years nonstop **(THE SWEAT AND TEARS, GROW AND EXPAND PHASE)**; then observe your manifestation of value you bring to the marketplace come true **(THE REAP PHASE)**. If you do your best, your greatest, at this, the riches you receive, the retirement money you attract to yourself, will never be too small to fit the person you've become.

So, when you decide it's time to retire you can check your social security, your fixed annuities (designate beneficiaries to leave your account to when you die, so money continues flowing to your loved ones), your trust(s), your pension(s), and your money from the marketplace (designate an executor for your will, power of attorneys, contingency beneficiaries) for the desired monthly income until you die.

BACKUP

Now you want to have backup money in place before you start any business. What might this look like you might ask? Very different for each person, of course. Let's say you envision a business making $60,000 a month, then put aside $60,000 a month.

Yes, I get it, you don't have $60,000 a month right now to put aside, but once the business gets underway put aside 25% of the profits as protection into a separate account; preferably in a different financial institution than your current accounts, to cover your bases.

Remember, I'm giving you where you need to get to, a target.

So, when or if the business fails, when there's a recession, God forbid a natural disaster, you can check your backup savings for the needed money to restore business as usual.

BUSINESS

Now you might be asking, what might this look like? We all need a business(es) just like we need housing, jobs, transportation, medical, retirement. You'd think the government, since they know this, would've perfectly put infrastructures in place to achieve this for everyone. We've been here, how long now, over 6000 years and we haven't figured out things yet. Come on now, we know exactly what needs to be done, but No, that will not happen, yet.

We are cursed to forever live under a government that takes a twentieth from its people and puts it in its own pocket; unless all mankind declare Jehovah's government is the one they need, and then it'll happen. So, until then, only a few, the 10% of people, get on with their lives.

I tell you now, wake up, get out of unconsciousness, get aware, get purposeful, get to self-actualization, get spiritually awakened, and get on with your life. Get to the person you really need to be, the person you were born to be, the person you were put on the planet to become.

Get on the Forbes list with your name as the richest media and entertainment giant, richest automotive giant, richest technology giant, richest finance and investments giant, richest fashion and retail giant, richest real estate giant, richest sports giant, richest whatever, just get a moving.

Maybe you're someone who everyone sees as a winner, but somehow now that you're being seen, you're above the radar, you're being noticed, all of a sudden you start losing, you give away your hand, your game, your power. Why is that? It's your own fear of yourself being a winner, that's what it is, that's all it is. You're not used to being a god, being a winner, being powerful, being invincible. Well, I am here to tell you, that's all you are, a winner, a god, invincible. So, the next time you feel seen, feel above the radar, feel watched, expectations of you winning grow, go ahead and WIN, think – you're gonna be your BEST, focus on your next move, don't be distracted by the people, strategize, go ahead and WIN, win big, win your BEST.

I am also speaking to the people who have not yet become passionate about something, possessed, driven, guided towards something. What are you waiting for? Homelessness to be illegal, what a thought! There should be a way so people running for office get no votes until homelessness is eradicated, no homeless person at all on the streets, nobody in the whole country votes until homelessness is gone; but I digress.

I listened to myself one day say, I want to be the best at this. I was speaking to making movies, films, my own films. I have never heard myself say I want to be the best at anything in my entire life. I got excellent grades in school, I repaired computers very well, but I'd never said those words before until I started passionately writing my own movies, driven to make my own films, of which I had no skill in, mind you. Then it hit me, and like I said I was already past age 30, it hit me, what I really wanted to do, liked to do, would do for the rest of my life, whether I made money or not, whether I failed or not. Why? Because although I enjoy the movies, although a few tears would flow when a really good one comes on, there were no movies on TV nor movies streaming that represented me, how I was, how I lived, how I related to people, the kind of heroes I enjoyed watching, the kind of love interests I enjoyed seeing.

You'll have your own why.

I am also speaking to the gig economy – independent contractors, on-call workers, temporary workers, part-time workers, freelance workers, leased workers – who form an integral informal part of our service industry. Your income may be from any number of gigs, which could run the gamut of either being seasonal or just plain sporadic. You're also a set of people who are extremely driven and motivated, or why else would you do what you do.

I remember working at various gigs at one point in my life, with no budget for food. I had to volunteer at churches near me, preparing meals, so I could have food for the week.

The fundamentals you'll receive during your read, will inspire you, motivate you, instill hope in you for the future. You'll start where you are, at $0 if needs be, and work your way to the person you need to be.

If you're in a full-time minimum wage situation, same. On June 14, 2023, the National Low Income Housing Coalition published – in no state, county, or city in the US can a full-time worker earning the local minimum wage come up with the costs for a two-bedroom apartment. A full-time worker in the US needs to make $28.58 an hour, on average, to afford rent on a modest two-bedroom apartment in their area and $23.67 an hour to afford a one-bedroom apartment.

When you're ready, and you're desiring to lift yourself out of your situation, this book will show you. Who knows, you may have already picked up a clue or two in this first chapter.

Once awakened, passionate, driven, the end result, the destination, is generating profit from what you do, from the legal income stream(s) that works for you. Whether it be from stocks, from your own dream or business idea, from properties, from the stock exchange, or whatever scenario(s) is unfolded you; preferably parents should guide their kids on this, generating profit at an early age. It's like I always say, 'Spend 30% of your money (when you can), the remaining 70% – 10% to emergency like charities, 25% to retirement like pensions, 25% to backup, and the extra 10% to business like your own business idea.' That's the extra 10% of your own money you're gonna use to generate profits using your own efforts.

Now once you've gotten your business up and running, hurry, build it fast fast fast into a large company, of over 500 employees, to survive this economic climate.

Then buy up multiple companies like American Businessman and philanthropist, Warren Buffet, one of the world's best-known investors, to expand your business into a conglomerate that strategically leads businesses for the future.

Your parents would've guided you the best they knew how, I hope you ate that up real good. Like my Mom was the one who said, "Save your money", and my Dad was the one who said, "Study hard"; then I met author George S. Clason, through his book The Richest Man in Babylon, who gave me the missing ingredient, "What you save must earn, and its children must earn." So, not only must you save your money, but you must make it earn for you, and its children must earn for you, profits, as well.

So, at age 30, when you're ready to choose not to work for anyone, you can check your business profits for the desired ongoing income and enjoy financial independence (the state at which an individual or household has sufficient wealth to live on without having to depend on income from some form of employment).

"Every man is not the same rat, running this rat race; every rat is different, and therefore, should be on his own path."

– ANONYMOUS

02 – THE TWELVE DIFFERENT PAINS

N ow there are twelve (12) different pains (not a conclusive list, but the most common ones) that will either hold you back or propel you forward towards your dreams depending on your perspective on them. I'm giving you my view on this, from my viewpoint, incorporating insights from astrologer Jeremy Neal, who published "Chiron In Aries Through The Houses", on his Chirotic Journal website.

First, allow me to clear up fear. What is fear? Fear is your spiritual self, recognizing that you're ready for the next great step, but your physical ego isn't yet ready or isn't yet sure. That's the definition of fear. There's no other definition. Reason being, fear isn't what really holds you back, it's you, your decision, your choice, that holds you back, if anything. Fear is not what we are talking about here.

Second, let me explain pain. What is the purpose of pain? Each and every one of us is born with a pain, a wound, a childhood perspective, some feeling of irrelevance, some area of life we feel weak in, we just can't shake it, we just feel disadvantaged in this area of life, or we feel protective in some area of life. The purpose of the pain is so we feel what another person goes through and can therefore be the best ones to offer the greatest help to them.

1. <u>One pain may be associated with your physical body or your personality.</u> Maybe you're not blessed with beauty, maybe you're maimed like athlete Jessica Long, maybe dwarfed like actor Peter Dinklage, maybe you suffered brain damage like coach Jim Kwik, maybe you were born with no vocal chords, maybe you stammered like American television host Steve Harvey, maybe you paint and write with your left foot like painter Christy Brown, maybe you were born blind and deaf like disability rights advocate Helen Keller, maybe you suffered Amyotrophic lateral sclerosis like physicist Stephen Hawking, maybe you're soft-spoken, or maybe you hated your Welsh accent like radio producer Philip H. Burton.

The pain forces you to dig deep within yourself, to research it, to figure out how you're gonna work with it, then it makes you aware of what you want (to do or be), propels you forward to express yourself at the highest level of spiritual awakening for all mankind to become, and finally ushers you towards the manifestation of your dreams where you are teacher, coach, or inspiration for others in some way.

2. <u>A second pain may be associated with your financial and material self-worth.</u> Maybe you're poor, maybe you're in a lot of debt, or maybe you feel financially and materially insignificant.

This pain will catapult you to creating your own financial significance, resulting in others learning from you how to improve their financial self-worth.

3. <u>A third pain may be associated with your</u>

<u>communication and intellect.</u>   Maybe you feel you don't have a voice, maybe you're not eloquent enough, maybe you have low intelligence, maybe you have poor handwriting, maybe you suffer from dyslexia, maybe you're autistic, or maybe your speech was painfully difficult like for human rights activist Malcolm X.

Malcolm X, with no formal education, literally studied the dictionary while in prison and used his incredible vocal power to assert a new political and social agenda in America.

4. <u>A fourth pain may be associated with establishing home, emotional security, and family dynasty.</u> Maybe you're homeless, maybe you feel a sense of irrelevance that your contribution to family does not matter, or maybe you feel emotionally insecure like nowhere is home for you.

The pain gives you the opportunity to improve your family dynamics and emotional security to become say a 'great Dad', a 'Father figure', an 'instrumental Provider' for your family and community.

5. <u>A fifth pain may be associated with your creativity or your self-expression.</u>   Maybe you've suffered a number of miscarriages, maybe you feel your sense of creativity is not worthy of recognition like music composer Ludwig van Beethoven, or maybe you feel inhibitions to self-express.

Whatever it is, when you start to work with whatever you have been given, whether you think it's a curse or a problem, it is then that your creativity begins to unfold. Just stay with it.

6. <u>A sixth pain may be associated with your occupation or your health.</u> Maybe you struggled getting acting jobs like stand-up comedian Jerry Seinfeld, maybe you've suffered a stroke like actress Sharon Stone, maybe you're a drug addict, maybe you're obese, maybe you're overlooking your fitness routines, maybe you're a liar and a thief, maybe you're lazy, maybe you're always late, maybe you're suicidal, maybe you're a serial killer, maybe you're a serial rapist, or maybe you feel your work is completely ignored.

In the case of Seinfeld, did you notice how he told his own type of jokes and gradually created his own career path?

For Sharon stone, notice how she has a great acting career, the stroke hit, then she started on a new life path. Illness makes you aware of your true life direction, what is truly important. They occur, illnesses occur, to give you an opportunity to listen to your body and make a roundabout turn – if you are working a job you know you hate and you do have something else you love doing, if you are stuck in an abusive relationship and you know you do deserve more, if you're eating really poorly and really do want to start a new fitness regime – the illness makes you listen to your body, so you make the necessary change.

The illness is a light switch telling you, showing you, reminding you, that the inclinations you have always been feeling/hearing in the back of your mind (the stuff that has been telling you, something isn't right about this life direction, something isn't kosher, this isn't right for me, this isn't what I really want to do with my life) are accurate, now it's time to follow them.

Any addiction, notice how it has a set timeframe that it lasts for. After that timeframe, do you notice how the addict changed? Whether by another individual's intervention or by some meeting or through being institutionalized in some way? The alcohol or the substance used numbs its users, so they don't have to deal with something or someone in their life, but after facing it, facing that someone or something, understanding it, accepting it, working with it, because it's all they have anyway, then comes the real change.

Serial killers and serial rapists are a different kettle of fish. They are a more specialized group of people who hone their craft and are on a mission. They have a routine, a schedule, something they must do, almost like they are obsessed (different from addicts), and they fully accept who they are. Researchers have all agreed these groups of people have some vendetta against so-called moralistic society, against a type of person, and/or against a type of political condition.

Serial killers and serial rapists would have to want more, more from what they're experiencing in life, more from the results of their own efforts. There would have to be something still insufficient about what they're currently doing, like it isn't really fully giving them what they're truly desiring, for change to begin. So, because they haven't yet seen this light, they just stick with what they know, and continue doing their routine.

This particular pain is a realization into the fact that the world or society or any person can never be the blame or the cause for whatever they feel has happened to them or whoever they feel wronged them. The only path forward is acceptance of self, YOU exactly as you are without BLAME. Rise to the level of seeing how you can work with what you've got. Listen to the other side of your mind, there is a direction that leads you to more, and how you know you're there, is in what you've manifested out into the world where you become an activist, coach, or inspiration in some special way.

Even thoughts of suicide are a clue to something, it's something or someone you're trying to escape from or no longer want to face. But look at how many people tried suicide and failed. The thought of suicide is not for you to actually commit it, it's for you to be aware of the truths involved. Look at the truth, accept it, accept whatever it says about you, then work with that, work with what you've been dealt with in life, work with it. Ask yourself, what can I do with this?

7. <u>The seventh pain may be associated with your business partners or your close relationships.</u> Maybe you feel powerless, maybe your needs are rendered insignificant in one-on-one relationships, maybe you feel an inability to assert yourself, maybe you've been bullied like stand-up comedian Chris Rock, maybe you've suffered domestic violence and physical abuse like singer Tina Turner, maybe you're being dominated, maybe you've experienced sexual abuse like American talk show host Oprah Winfrey, or maybe you suffered mental abuse from your father like filmmaker Tyler Perry.

This pain will guide you to find a means of creating your own significance in close relationships while showing you how to give people more freedom of self-expression and self-assertion. Since you feel the pain the most, as a result of having powerful authority figures over you and being restricted when it comes to being yourself, you are the best one to offer the greatest help in the area of sensitive and empathetic expression of authoritative power.

8. <u>The eighth pain may be associated with other people's resources or your sex drive.</u>   Maybe you're in fights over inheritance, maybe you have no will power, maybe you're a gold-digger, maybe you're a master manipulator, maybe you're impotent, maybe you're frigid in intimate relationships, maybe you're a sex addict, or maybe you suffered a sense of sexual worthlessness like magazine publisher Hugh Hefner.

This pain gives you the capacity to develop your own money, your own sexual power.

9. <u>The ninth pain may be associated with higher learning and your philosophy of life.</u>   Maybe you're under-qualified and inexperienced in your vocational life, maybe you struggle to develop a meaningful and supportive philosophy of life, or maybe you're born with mental disabilities and suffer learning difficulties.

This pain will generate sorts of persons like, for instance, educator Maria Montessori activist for mentally retarded children.

10. <u>The tenth pain may be associated with your vocation or your reputation.</u>   Maybe you feel your status is unrecognized, or maybe you feel your greatest achievements are ignored by others.

This pain propels you to a slow and steady progress towards success where you become a stalwart and reliable authority figure in society.

11. <u>The eleventh pain may be associated with friends or social groups.</u>   Maybe you feel you have no friends, maybe you feel you're a loner, maybe you feel your genius and uniqueness remains unnoticed, or maybe you feel you don't fit in with the in-crowd.

Make no mistake, this pain produces leaders who fight for new social orders or specific causes.

12. <u>The twelfth pain may be associated with your unconscious or your dreams.</u>   Maybe you're a day dreamer like author J.K. Rowling, maybe you're a mystic like author Caroline Myss, maybe you repress your emotions, maybe you're a poetic, maybe you're confined to an institution in some way, or maybe you're a psychic.

But whatever you do, the pain destines you to change your perspective on it, to stop holding yourself back, and to begin seeing that there is another way forward using the pain, in the greatest way, in service to all mankind.

Therefore, everything, every excuse, every situation not moving you forward, every crises, every stumbling block, every failure, is a symptom of one or more of the twelve (12) different pains, just waiting for you to come out of its cycle, and decide what you want to do. Lazy, stuck in a bad relationship, feeling worthless, hate your job, not making enough money, racist, procrastinating, narcissist, suicidal, addict, not fit, stammering, autistic, not creative, undergoing constant tax audits, no college degree, no faith, poor branding in the marketplace, disloyal friends, stuck in the past, slow reader, stuck in a rut, writers' block – ALL ARE SYMPTOMS OF ONE OR MORE OF THE TWELVE (12) DIFFERENT PAINS – waiting for you to come out of it, and decide what you want to do.

The eye opener for me was making 6 figures at age 50 and COULDN'T EVEN MAX OUT THE PENSION ACCOUNTS the company offered to secure a retirement. I spent only 30% of my income and wasn't rich. 6 figures just wasn't cutting it as it used to, but when I saw I could be #1 richest media and entertainment giant on the 2033 Forbes list, producing my own films that represent people similar to me, everything changed. The pain forced me to remove every and all limits, I had on my ability to assert myself.

03 – TIMEFRAMES FOR EVERYTHING

I hope to reveal during your read that every man is not the same rat, running this rat race; every rat is different, and therefore, should be on his own path.

The current misconception is that schools should teach you everything, but if schools taught you everything, you would never gain in value. Gaining value comes from constantly improving your knowledge and skills. What society should just accept is that schools provide the basics and it's up to individuals to now be responsible for their own skills-set development.

The rat race just amasses more automobiles. Notice that? We can't all be doctors, lawyers, engineers. The more I can help everyone I come in contact with, become rich early, the less traffic there'll be on the roads because rich people fly they don't drive. That's my goal, everyone rich early.

Once you've got a handle on your pain(s) and you're in pursuit of your dreams, there are timeframes for everything under the Sun. Whilst some things can happen immediately, it is important to bear in mind, some things require a specific timeframe before they can happen. For example, there are timeframes for work, timeframes to reap, timeframes for a recession, timeframes to be profitable, timeframes to have a loss, timeframes to recover from loss, timeframes for birth, and each timeframe must be completed before another timeframe can begin.

For example,

- 6-7 years, the timeframe to put in the work, create, develop, bear fruit, before any achievement can be realized, e.g., before reaping the rewards of your sweat and tears, before recovering from a recession, before profitability,

- 10-25 years, the timeframe for institutionalization e.g., before you fully pay for criminal offenses or before fully recovering from drug related offenses,

- 30 years, the timeframe for next stage advancement e.g., before birth of adulthood

- 50 years, the timeframe for mid-life strength of character,

- 60 years, the timeframe for mentorship role and giving of wisdom,

- 70 years, the timeframe for maturity and good sustained health.

04 – THINK TWICE
BEFORE YOU ATTACK
A WOMAN

In the past, a lonely road, a female walks home alone, she's followed, attacked, left raped. Now, in a time where women are more skilled, there will be no more of this. It would read –

A lonely road, a female walks home alone, the thought of following her wouldn't even enter your mind, because if you did follow her and attempted to attack her, your throat would be slit with a legally carrying weapon/knife that she would not be afraid to use in defense of her life and/or property.

You're at a charging station, you see a lone female charging her automobile, the thought of going over to her wouldn't even enter your mind, especially if your intent is to harm her. You would know that you would lose your life in that moment; it's not worth it.

A husband is upset with his wife, he raises his hand, swings it in the direction of her face to slap her, she blocks the slap, breaks his wrist; no more where that came from.

So, no more domestic violence calls to 911, no more batter bruised females in shelters, no more women accepting batters and bruises out of fear; women change the landscape of physical crimes against themselves.

A special note to female security guards: Hair should not extend below the bottom edge of the collar. Hair should be arranged so as not to interfere with vision in any way. Hair should not be left hanging down in a ponytail hairstyle, for safety reasons.

At one point I thought to myself, it would be great to have a world where no physical bodily crimes or blue-collar crimes existed. Why not white-collar crimes instead, no one would be murdered? White-collar crimes are on the rise; but when someone or something wipes out your bank account digitally or steals your identity remotely or holds your organization ransom maliciously, it can be just as devastating as a blue-collar crime against you.

So, here's a theory, prisons are a place the perpetrator FEELS THE HURT he causes his victim(s), not a place to rest for a time to go back into the world to do the same thing to other victims. When perpetrators know they'll feel the hurt they cause another person, chances are they won't harm anyone again. Now if a perpetrator murders someone, we're not saying murder the perpetrator, No. But a well-designed scheme where perpetrators feel the hurt caused will ensure remorse sets in. Prisons that force you to change your thinking, change your mind, elevate you to self-actualization, inspire spiritual awakening.

We are all heading to the destination of spiritual awakening, we are. So, why not reform prisons in that manner, so that we all get to that destination.

Don't tell me there's no money to do it, better you say that's not where your focus is currently. But look at the state of the world, don't you think your focus had better change?

So many assaults against person(s) are happening now and happening even more so at an alarming rate because there's no real penalty, no remorse, no real institutions of reform. Where is the boundary that once was? Where I respected my neighbors' personal space? Cops never had to brutally arrest persons before like they do now. I'm saying, go back to **RESPECT**, respect a person's space, respect a person's wishes, respect a person's rights, respect a person's body, a person's property and family. If you want something that badly go work for it, the old fashion sweat and tears way where the feeling of gratification when you're done is so satisfying.

It is my opinion, the seventh pain is the most severe, since it's the pain that deals with assaults from another person.

Which brings us to the topic of bullying, domestic violence, and being dominated (sexually or otherwise). Reframe your mind to the view that you, maybe in another life, asked for this circumstance to come into your life.

YOU want to stand up to this person bullying you and/or this person committing domestic violence against you and/or this person dominating you, otherwise your life would be different. See that there is the possibility you have and can bully someone else, you can be violent if pushed too far, see where you may have dominated someone else somewhere or you may want to be dominant yourself; then you'll begin to see life from a completely different perspective. If you can go, even a step further, as far as realizing that you are actually upset with, even possibly jealous of, your bullier/attacker/oppressor for doing exactly what you want (to do or be), then something will open up in your mind and life and even in your actions that will cause the way you see your bullier/attacker/oppressor to change. It is YOU who wants to be an aggressor, be a fighter, be strong (sexually or otherwise). You just attracted those persons into your life to force you to start doing what you always wanted to do. The fight will be fierce, but the result – priceless once achieved.

So, if you want to get rid of a bully, start being that side of yourself. Listen to the side of yourself who is begging to come out. Do you want to be a star? Do you want to get all the girls? Do you want to win at sports? Go win at those things and the bullying will disappear because you're already doing it. The bullier just attacks those who are weak, if you don't see yourself as weak anymore there's nothing to attack.

If you want to get rid of a domestically violent partner, start being that side of yourself, it's there. What part of you wants to be a fighter? What part of yourself has very demanding emotions asking to be let out? What part of yourself wants wants wants to be independent? Listen to yourself. Go win at those things – Join a debate team, argue and win that argument; Go do jujitsu, fight and win that fight; You have a talent or a dream, do your own business, go platinum with your own album. You're going to be so far from that attacker you won't even remember who they were.

And, if you want to get rid of being dominated (sexually or otherwise), you guessed it, start being that side of yourself. Listen to the side of yourself begging to come out. Do you want to be more expressive and be heard? Do you want to be authoritative?

Do you want to take charge in bed? Do those things and you won't feel as though you're being dominated in the same way.

So, women put your hands up, block those attackers' fists, snatch back your baby from those kidnappers, say no to staying down to any rapist, whatever you have to do to protect your life and/or your body and/or your property.

Honestly though, if we could stop attacking people, generally. Respect yourself. But it doesn't stop there. The person being attacked and the person attacking both need to start over. Find the light at the end of the tunnel. Accept that what is happening now is, a turning point, a wall, a precipice, telling you it's time to change, time to recognize a new beginning, a new path you need to take, a new road to go on. No more living life this old way. That's what you should be interpreting this circumstance in your life to mean – not be victim nor oppressor unconsciously forever.

05 – STOP BEING
A LATE A$$

You've never been late for anything, it's the people around you who think you're always late, right? It's just 30 mins, they can wait 30 mins more, right? You've tried everything, it is what it is, right?

It is my opinion, the sixth pain sometimes appears in mediocre forms, but still must be dealt with.

Learn how to ALWAYS be on time. How do I do it? I can tell you it's like relationships, you have to work at it.

Ok, so you have an 8:30 am staff meeting. How drab, right? You watch everybody else, no one else is even budging in the direction of the conference room. You check the clock, it's 8:29 am. You tell yourself, you've got time. Now it's 8:35 am. You drag yourself in the direction of the conference room. You say morning to everyone else walking into the meeting late too, and as you walk in, you observe a few employees who arrived early.

This has been your pattern all your life. Late for church, late for school, late paying bills, late on your mortgage, late on dates, late for appointments, always late.

It's like, I was commending my Dad, six days before the year 2023 Fathers' Day, that he's still with the same woman. Bill Gates and many others caused their breakup in the middle of their old age. 'Why would anyone do that to themselves?', I would ask myself. Wives being so very understanding in these areas these days, especially wealthier wives, that is. What husbands have forgotten is that if they want more from their wives, they've got to do more. Remember, you were the one who SAW her, CHOSE her, and she said YES, right? Now, she has stopped putting out because you haven't done anything new with yourself for her to even find you even remotely attractive anymore. So, you have to start over, Sir, pretend you're SEEING her for the very first time. Start working out, get a promotion, learn a new language, learn a new skill, start CHOOSING her all over again, shower her with gifts like you did in the early years, she'll say YES again like in the beginning. She'll start fixing up her hair again, because you attract to you who you are. You attract to yourself the new person you are becoming. That's it, husbands. Fix YOURSELVES up, if you want wives to get back to putting out. Don't forget wives keep score too.

So, the same for being prompt. If you want to be early, if you want to be on time, you've got to do more. Wake up earlier, get two alarm clocks or watches if needs be, go to bed early, set the time 30 minutes early if you have to. Whatever it takes. Pay for a wake-up service. In other words, start saying to yourself, I will be 30 minutes early to everywhere I go. Put in the work. Wake up 30 minutes earlier than normal. Tell yourself, you're a 30-minute early man, go to work 30 minutes early, go to that staff meeting 30 minutes early. Get in your automobile 30 minutes earlier than usual, so you can get to that date 30 minutes early. You have to set it in your mind – I'm a 30-minute early man, I'm never late. Do everything in your power to never be late, not even by a second. Why? You attract who you are, and you need to get to the person you really need to be.

Now, what does the research say? It says it's arrogance, time blindness, zero value of self why people are always late. I say it's just, you reel the toilet paper from the bottom, I reel it from the top.

So, where do we go from here? Ask yourself the question, **WHAT WOULD YOU LIKE SOMEONE ELSE TO DO FOR YOU?** You are the host of the staff meeting, would you like your employees to straddle in late? You wait for your date to show, would you like him/her to arrive late? You order dinner, would you like the delivery service to be late? You own a bank that collects mortgage payments, would you like late payments from your customers? No, no one would.

Then ask yourself, Is there another underlying reason why I'm always late? Why am I always late? Why do I allow myself to always be late? What do I get out of it? There is something going on there. You have a philosophy, and this philosophy is guiding you to always be late. What is that philosophy? What new philosophy can you now live by? Specifically, now, because you need to get to the person you really need to be, the person you were born to be, the person you were put on the planet to become.

Go back to your dreams. What were they? Put pen to paper. Write down what you want. What you want to do. Then start doing it. It's possible you lost your way disguised as being a late ass, but no more. Now you're ready for more, now your eyes are open to new possibilities.

One of our greatest challenges is keeping our mind on our highest goal. We'll aim at $20,000,000 profits, then later shrink it to $2,000,000, saying to ourselves, 'That's more manageable, I can achieve that'. Reach high when you set your dream's goal. It's not for you to understand how it will manifest, it's for you to work towards it and let the universe do the rest. You don't plant watermelon seeds with the goal of watermelons and then say, 'No they're too large, I prefer tangerines, those I can manage.' No, you just plant, put in the work, dream your highest, and allow the universe to conjure up the means by which you will arrive at your dream(s).

I always felt powerless around very powerful people, like I couldn't be myself, like I shouldn't be myself around them – my parents, authority figures, powerful men – until I realized I, I, was a powerful person myself. Powerful people saw me as an authority figure, someone who they were even intimidated by or easily influenced by. Nothing came for me though until I was past age 30. I just kept studying in school, from Kindergarten to University. Friends would call me 'sponge' because I would just suck up the lessons so quickly and pass the exams so fast. It was at age 40 that I got the first inkling of an idea of what I wanted to do, what I wanted to become, then I noticed myself writing it down on paper, a plan, visualizing it. It wasn't until the dream got clearer that the details got more specific, and then it began unfolding to me how I would work towards this dream. Man did I start hurrying. You begin to realize it's so much to do in so little time.

It's the same for you, start where you are. So, you're a late ass, accept it. But now, what else can you do, with that, out there in the world, for the public, for profit, to help someone else? Which, if you haven't figured it out by now, is really helping you in the long run.

Remember, you attract to you who you are. You attract to yourself the new person you are becoming. Never before in the history of mankind has there ever been a time like the present, where YOU need to get to the person you really need to be.

Put in the work, do it for that 6 years nonstop. That's you building, creating, and developing the value in yourself. It is this value already created within you, that attracts the wealth you're worth.

Earn profits from that wealth, then earn more profits from those profits also, according to your desire.

06 – SOCIAL NORMS YOU DON'T CARE FOR

SHOCK YOUR BODY

So, you're fat. The world is obviously gonna end then. No, own it, some curves are good. I bet an attacker would think twice before approaching you. The sky's no limit.

Now, you're obese. Doctors have already warned you about your health. Yes, this too has a new window of opportunity – whiter teeth, you eat great, best physique, whatever your deepest desires are.

Use the formula, what is that one thing you do when no one else is looking, what do you want (to do or be), make a list of what you're going to do in pursuit of this dream, whatever you have to do to generate profit from the public, and set the highest goal, put in the work, do it for that 6 years nonstop, attract the wealth you're worth. Then make what you save from that wealth earn you profits, and those profits earn you more profits. You'll never be the same again.

Start brushing your teeth with fluoride twice a day, that's in addition to regular brushing. Watch the teeth naturally renew.

Accept that you eat great, right now, where you stand or sit, shout, "I eat great". Tell yourself, I eat great, always, every day, I eat great. Notice the changes begin to happen in this area.

You can't follow social norms or even your own ideas of what fitness regime to use, you have to follow a class, a mentor, a trainer. The best physique comes from doing what you would never normally do, that's the only way to get results from any fitness program. If it's easy to run, then that's not what you should go do for your fitness regime. If it's easy to cycle with a buddy, then that's not what you should go do for your fitness regime. You've got to do what's hard, what you would never normally put your body through, you've got to shock your body and your muscles. A combat boot camp class, an extreme workout fitness video, a professional trainer. Three (3) times a week for the next 6 years nonstop, but it must be for profit, from the public. THINK, use your brain.

Offer fitness products for sale, start a podcast to garner viewers, host fitness classes for people like you, sew fitness gear, buy a gym get 2% fee off total assets 20% off all profits, and/or do your own business idea that may not have anything to do with fitness. Observe the new person you've become.

One last point, but by no means least, good sustained health with rejuvenated physique comes after 70 years of consistently looking after yourself. Why aren't we in the gym then in our 90s?

HOLIDAYS

I have said No to friends who invite me to their homes for Thanksgiving or Christmas. Over the years, I've just never enjoyed it. At their homes, relatives come over, sit, eat, never get up again, especially the men, then leave.

For that very reason, I no longer go to people's homes. It's just sit, eat, more food to eat, and nothing to do before or even after eating. Run, play, a game, sing, dance, something... nothing.

I'm that person with the Charades, Connect 4, Jenga games ready to play. I want to DO something when I get to your home, I want to dance to music, I want to play football/soccer, I want to play bun eating contests, beer drinking contests, tap you're it, I want to play monopoly, scrabble, uno, you name it.

Let me be clear, I enjoy food just as the next man, but I do not want to sit, eat, watch TV all day, clean your home, wash your dishes (so ensure you use plastic plates), nor cook, the same I already do at my own home. Let me know what you prefer I bring, I usually take champagne or something similar when going to family and friends.

CONVERSATIONS

And boy, do I like the quiet, at work, at home, when I'm driving, with a Lyft or Uber driver. People seem to need to talk all the time to take up the time. I feel if you're going to just talk to kill time, then the conversation isn't really meaningful then, is it?

You're just killing time. I prefer to have meaningful conversations, ask the right questions, that reveal to me how interesting that individual really is who I'm speaking with, because everyone has something special to teach us all.

You'll have your own quirks.

HEALTH

I am a stickler for not holding anything in, especially when it comes to the smooth and efficient functioning of the body I was given. I am a big fan of getting things out of my body as fast as it is willing to leave. My mindset is, the faster it gets outside me, the less gets clogged up inside.

So, my job is to make the necessary accommodation as best as I possibly can to get stuff moving. If he has to pee, find the nearest lavatory wherever it may be; if he has to expel, raise that left butt-cheek if needs be; if he has to poo, hell yeah, exit that executive meeting, get that job done pronto.

This I recommend to everyone, don't hold anything in, allow your day-to-day actions to add to the well-functioning flow of your body's fluids, gases, solids, cells, organs, and bones.

PLAY

Play is vital, working 24/7 is not. When last have you, as an adult, played? Really played with your spouse, anyone? Chased them around the bed, the dining table, the house?

Go back to playing more. It reduces stress, it increases your sex life, it connects you back to your kid-like self. Life is not just eat, work, eat, work, maybe a vacation or two. Life is fun, so play more as you go through the process.

CELLPHONES

I have stopped buying cellphones. I'll wait until the size gets back down smaller with batteries that last a minimum of 30 days again.

I say that to say, don't pay attention to social norms, don't follow the crowd, also watch what you do and say socially, it all affects your ultimate journey to your dreams.

You want to keep your mind on your highest goal, your body prepped for your best work, don't let anything distract you, keep people around who enforce your goals, who are, too, awakened spiritually, heading to their truest/highest self.

"There is no such thing as something for nothing."

– NAPOLEON HILL, AUTHOR OF MASTER KEY

07 – GETTING DOWN TO WORK

So, where do I start? I'm all confused, too much information, I don't wanna, it's too much work, I don't have all the knowledge, is it Friday yet? Are all responses to leave you broke at age 40 or, worse, broke at age 60. Let's agree, it's much better to choose to do the needed work, than be forced by life, illness, or karma to do the needed work, right?

I had already written two (2) movie scripts, my lovely friend and retired English Teacher helped me format and proofread the stories. Then I found myself aiming high, higher than ever before – we'll make 48,000 films in two (2) years, create 48,000 albums in two (2) years, write 48,000 books in two (2) years. I began doing what American entrepreneur, author, and motivational speaker, Jim Rohn said, "Work harder on yourself than you do at your job". I taught myself the animation software, Blender. I hunted down audio recording equipment and studios. I looked up best-selling self-help books. I stopped wasting time. Every minute I had on the train, every minute I had at work, every minute I had at home, I wrote an extra line in my book, I recorded an extra melody for my album, I created an extra scene of my movie.

So, I have my accountability person a retired English Teacher, my emergency contact person a Cafeteria Worker, all I need now is my MASTERMIND ALLIANCE group, according to American self-help author Napoleon Hill of the book Master Key, two or more persons who work in perfect harmony for the attainment of a definite purpose. I contacted people on craigslist to animate my movie, streaming services online to sell my music, self-publishing websites to sell my books, in order to form my alliance. I began writing out a schedule of what needed to be produced and by when. Some days, I was excited with my progress, other days frustrated with my computer speed, others annoyed with Blender, some days I was sleepy, other days I was stuck couldn't move forward, others I had so much energy, but they never said it was going to be always fun nor exciting. It's work, that's what it's supposed to feel like. So, I just kept going, kept working, kept persevering.

I found that people who kept second guessing themselves or kept needing to know how their big dream was going to happen, didn't really want that dream; basically, they weren't really feeling it deeply. People who really wanted their dreams, really did want it, really felt it, hell or high water couldn't stop them. No problem though, just re-evaluate yourself if you're not quite there yet, find or feel what you truly really want, and go after it. When you really want your dream or really want what you want to do, the HOW won't matter. Whatever you do, you'll **HOLD THAT DREAM IN YOUR THOUGHTS UNTIL YOU GET IT**, if you think about or focus on anything else for any reason, then that which you focus upon is what you'll receive, that's according to Australian television writer, producer, and author Rhonda Byrne of the book The Secret (available as a movie as well).

Don't allow illnesses to come upon you. You have the capability of looking at that illness and getting rid of it, by having in your mind the new person you wish to become, focusing on that new person, and commanding the illness to leave you, to leave your body, is the power of choice you have. REMEMBER: The universe is standing by awaiting your every request.

So, focus, buckle down, put in the work, get it done, nonstop, don't waste any time; it's author Napoleon Hill, in his book Master Key, who wrote, "There is no such thing as something for nothing".

RELATIONSHIPS

Now, if you're married, I understand things are going to be a bit different – loved ones are now involved, responsibilities are numerous, partnership win-wins are paramount – you're going to have to work together on this. I'm not married, not yet anyway, and so, let me interject something here for a moment, any advice or recommendation I may impart during your read in no way suggests nor confirms that I'm an expert at marriage or relationships or dating, there are just a few things I've observed over my 50 years of existence on this planet that has taught me a few things...That's all, that's all it is. Plus, it's actually quite simple, people who are divorced do not want to work together, people who are married want to work together, there's no secret, it's that simple. He decided he wants in, she decided she wants in, you make up your mind, it's a decision, no secret.

You have to want to give more than you receive to the other person, already knowing (in the back of your mind) you are fully taken care of by the universe once you do that. That's why most relationships can't and won't work. Both partners are seeking for themselves. It will never work, because what is always there is the fear that once one partner gives his/her all, the other partner will step on that and never give back the same in return. But the fear here is your spiritual self, recognizing you're ready to give more than you receive, but your physical ego isn't yet ready. When you give more than you receive, the universe works to ensure you receive all you give, it always does. **YOU WILL ALWAYS RECEIVE IN THE EXACT PROPORTION THAT WHICH YOU GIVE OUT INTO THE WORLD**. I guarantee you. If you give nothing, you get nothing. If you love hard, you get lots of love, kindness, respect coming back at you. That's just the Law of the Universe.

Do a test for yourself, give only half your best and watch how the people around you give back their efforts in that same proportion. I did a test once, I did a number of tests actually. I used to give away all my wrinkled up and old $1, $5, $10 bills whenever someone asked me for change, and then one day I sort of noticed every time I received money it was always a raggedy, torn, or old dollar bill. Then I started always giving my crispest and best bills to people. Now, every time I receive money it's always a crisp and new dollar bill. Now, you try it, always give your best and watch how the people around you give back their best in the exact same proportion.

Here's another scenario, you find you have thoughts of cheating on your partner, you will begin to see and observe clues or signs that suggest to you your partner is also cheating on you. Now when you have nothing but good intentions for your partner, I repeat, nothing but good intentions, you will only see the same good intentions coming back at you.
I would recommend walking away from cheating partners. You may decide to keep that relationship going for a number of reasons, for any number of years to come, it's your decision, but when a partner chooses to cheat they have already decided to invest elsewhere (i.e. 1. choosing not to improve him/herself and 2. deciding that their current relationship is no longer a good investment) and here's what I mean.

Remember, when a relationship starts, one partner decides this is a good investment and so is willing to do the work that it requires. A price is paid in the form of dating, chivalry, getting to know each other, introduction to family (for this one, if the person is the right choice). The other partner assesses the level of investment, sets a high score when their needs are being met, then intimacy is given. As time goes by, as the first partner continues to reduce investment in the relationship, the second partner's score will also show a reduction causing intimacy to be withdrawn.

It is at this point that the first partner will make a decision, do I continue to invest in my current relationship, or do I invest in a new relationship? To invest in a new relationship doesn't require the first partner to change in any way, develop any new skills, expand their thinking, improve upon themself, start going to the gym, get a promotion, or anything. So, the first partner would usually choose to start a new relationship, but it's just sex understand that.

What I'm saying is, the cheating partner opted for not adding more value to him/herself. And that's what they call, in the industry, a red flag. In other words, the first partner decided to no longer give more than they receive to their partner. And maybe the second partner was the one who fell down on giving their best in the first place, but that's not a relationship, though, anyone should be in.

I'm not saying the second partner is a bad investment, there'll always be good investors, but walk away, move on, surround yourself with people who are similar to who you are, who want to grow and expand, who want to live at their highest level. And for that reason, for that very reason, I don't believe in the one and only, the true one, the only one, the soulmate, because you can make a relationship work with anybody. Just use the Law of the Universe.

Men, keep investing in your relationship, it is a price that you must pay to get what you desire. Women, are always keeping score and when the score is too low, it's time to up your level of investment. Expand yourself, gain more knowledge and skills, learn a new trade, own a new company, choose the current relationship, give more in order to receive more, use your creativity, surprise your partner for a whole week. Both partners decide what they want in the relationship, there's no secret.

When you do not give more than you receive to the other partner, so many other things begin to break down in the relationship:-

- The men complain, 'She's a nag'
- The women complain, 'He does nothing around the house'
- The men complain, 'She treats me like a child'
- The women complain, 'He's like a child'

You have to want to give more than you receive to the other partner, so respect comes in, and you'll hear things like:-

- The men brag, 'She gives me time with the boys'
- The women brag, 'He always takes out the trash'
- The men brag, 'She surprised me with a blow job on my birthday'
- The women brag, 'He bought me the biggest diamond necklace I've ever seen'

Both partners are *NOT* seeking for themselves. Both partners are always growing in the relationship, that's the only way I see a relationship will work. If either partner stays the same, the relationship will begin to die, at some point. Each partner has to grow in the relationship.

We, however, do need a new way to view marriage though, maybe in the form of a 7-year contractual agreement. Our lives are evolving so fast, that from the look of things, to still be bound by the regular 'til death do us part' contract, is getting more and more difficult.

Men and women, go back to holding out a bit, get to know one another properly, it's never too old-fashioned. Even American television host, producer, actor, stand-up comedian, and author Steve Harvey of the book Act Like A Lady Think Like A Man, states women set the bar too low giving away benefits way before a 90-day probationary period is even over, the necessary time needed to get the full details on who the man really is and what are his intentions. Men set the bar too low also, in my opinion, not respecting themselves enough. Please, assess the full portfolio of the woman and meet the full scope of her needs. My recommendation is a 90-day probationary period for all dates, a 7-year contractual agreement (which includes a prenup clause) for all marriages, and a 90-day close-out period for all divorces to appropriately split assets.

The dating scene has gotten even more confusing, you don't even know who wants whom anymore. I don't even know who, for example, non-binary persons are attracted to, say I wanted to set them up with someone. Who are they interested in? What are their preferences? You see what I mean, we have to go back to holding out a bit, get to know one another properly, dig deeper below the surface (especially for a long-term investment), think about how this person will appear to you after the 'love phase' is over, Will you still be willing to think of their needs first over yours? Will you still find them interesting? Will you still want to be around them?

For the ladies, author Steve Harvey of the book Act Like A Lady Think Like A Man, suggests you should ask, during the dating phase, five (5) questions to determine if he's serious and whether you are in his plans:-

1. What are your short-term goals?
2. What are your long-term goals?
3. What are your views on relationships? (For example, is his relationship with his mother normal?)
4. What do you think about me?
5. What do you feel about me?

Once married, you're going to have to work together on the dream, you're going to have to be on the same page, you're going to have to fight the same fight, reach the same goal, motivate like basketball coaches, and finally win together like it truly supposed to be.

08 – THE LOTTERY

In the event you should win the lottery, during the process, here are some rules you should follow after you win.

1. Be guided when you go about choosing your numbers, don't force it. It's usually what you wouldn't expect.

2. Continue putting in the work towards your dreams, continue working. You still need to generate profits from your own efforts and gain the value (in yourself) equivalent to the winnings you just won.

3. Before collecting, choose a law firm to represent you in all dealings.

4. Before collecting, choose an accounting firm to handle your IRS paperwork.

5. Before collecting, choose an investment firm to create a trust for you, to collect the winnings for you, to keep your name anonymous.

6. Choose the lump sum payment, so you get the current value of your money on the day. Choosing the annuity payment, inflation after 30 years, will erode the value of your winnings.

7. Change your address and contact information by

relocating, and choose an executive security firm for security protection where applicable.

8. Immediately budget your winnings – attorney/accountant/advisor flat fees and taxes, emergency fund, retirement fund, backup money (I recommend this be 25% of your after-tax winnings), stock, your business idea, commercial real estate, stock exchange, allocate exactly how much you want to leave to family in a trust with clear guidelines when it should be spent and that it should be spent on commercial real estate (this one, just my preference) or other similar risk free ventures that return profits – then, stick to that do not alter.

9. Budget also for liability insurance, key person insurance, and disability insurance to fully protect In the event other insurances run out.

10. Help others, plan on donating to charities you're very close to.

11. Continue conducting training workshops, podcasts, webinars, and/or conferences in the attainment of your dreams.

12. Only spend your winnings after it has earned you profits, dividends, or interests, then earn more profits, dividends, and interests from those returns also, according to your desire.

A special note to joint ticket holders: A lottery ticket copy should be in the hands of all parties involved. A written statement copy with each party's contribution should be available to all parties involved, so it's objectively clear the proportion to split winnings. The original lottery ticket should be signed and put in an agreed upon secure place.

"We get paid for bringing value to the marketplace; The way that you become rich is by focusing on making yourself better."

– JIM ROHN, AUTHOR OF THE KEYS TO SUCCESS

09 – CONSEQUENCE OF NOT BEING RICH EARLY

THE SIX BLESSINGS

When you get to the person you really need to be, the person you were born to be, the person you were put on the planet to become, you may enjoy the riches that come from accepting who YOU are (after looking inside yourself), deciding what you truly WANT (to do or be), holding that dream in your THOUGHTS until you get it, and putting in the work developing yourself that brings VALUE to the marketplace.

According to American self-help author Napoleon Hill of the book Master Key, there are six (6) blessings derived from being rich early:-

- Sound Health
- Peace of Mind
- Work you Love of your own choice
- Freedom from Fear and Worry
- Positive Mind

- Financial and Material Riches of your own choice and quantity

THE SIX BURDENS

Y ou must, however, suffer the consequences that come from neglecting to get to the person you really need to be, the person you were born to be, the person you were put on the planet to become.

According to American self-help author Napoleon Hill of the book Master Key, the six (6) burdens ensued from *NOT* being rich early are:-

- Ill Health
- Regret and Disappointment
- Indecision and Doubt
- Fear and Worry
- Envious Mind
- Poverty and Want

FINANCIAL INDEPENDENCE
IS THE GOAL THEN

Financial independence is the state at which an individual or household has sufficient wealth to live on without having to depend on income from some form of employment.

Don't be mistaken, financial success, riches or wealth, must also encompass – well-balanced self-care, mutually satisfying relationships and being fully a part of a responsible thriving community.

WHAT IS YOUR MONEY FOR

Decide. What is your money for?

A long-time ago, I remember asking myself, "Why do I work?", "Why do I get up and go to work every morning?".

Then I decided, I wanted the money to have my meals delivered to my home automatically, I wanted the money to have my laundry delivered to my home automatically. That's why I worked, among other reasons.

I later decided I wanted my work, the work I do through a well-designed system, to generate money automatically, so I didn't have to work as hard. Why? I liked automation, things done for me automatically, so I could focus on other more important things;

Like enjoying meaningful companionship(s) throughout my days and throughout my routine social life.

SO WHAT THEN IS LIFE'S PURPOSE

Your life's purpose is YOUR decision to do or be a particular thing or person respectively. The universe does not shower upon you your purpose, you don't wake up in the morning and it falls into your lap.

You actually make a decision and say to the universe this is what I'm going to be doing with my life, and so, that then becomes your life's purpose, for some their life's mission, others their social cause.

10 – PASS ON
A LEGACY

Wealth should be passed to the next generation and to their generation after that, based on their family tree.

Keep the wealth in the family through wills, trusts, prenups. Teach family members how to acquire wealth, how to have wealth work for them, and how to pass wealth to the next generation.

I would like to leave a legacy for my nieces, for their nieces' nieces, and for their nieces after that.

Wouldn't that be great! Why do families, come up, are forced to work excruciating hours every day for the rest of their lives, their kids, come up, forced to work excruciating hours every day for the rest of their lives, the same for their kids and their kids' kids? It's time to stop that pattern.

Everyone has the choice of work he/she wishes to do, it's the right of every man. Everyone has the choice of the way he/she wants his/her life to be, it's the right of every man. DON'T FORGET THAT!

So, stop prodding along 'richless', as a society, like there's not enough riches to go around. Get some money under your belts for your families and your families' families. Get back to being a hero, a leader, a visionary. Stop lying around on the streets, doing nothing. Get some money under your belts for your children and your children's children... Who's with me? Can I hear an Amen!

11 – MAKE A DECISION WORKSHOP: THE FORMULA

I found that people won't make a choice until what they want to be, or offer is the BEST. People won't make a decision on what they want (to do or be) unless it's the BEST they're going after. Notice that? Because unless it's the BEST

- They're not going to read the books to get better,
- They're not going to stay up all night to go the extra mile, and
- They're not going to add the extra value to their customers.

When you're going after the BEST, notice, you don't even need as much sleep anymore, you don't even need as much food anymore. It's like really becoming spiritual where you no longer need physical desires met.

Notice how Jesus started his life's mission of gathering disciples around age 28-30? He was awakened spiritually – walking on water, turning water to wine, healing the sick – as early as age 30.

As a society, we're making this choice too late in life, we're entering this awakening phase too late in life (especially since we're all dying earlier and earlier). We should be spiritually awakened already by age 30. The equivalent of being, like I said in earlier chapters, retired by age 30, so you may share and help others early, manifest your life's purpose early, enjoy the blessings of being rich early.

Life is not the everyday existence that you're living right now, that's not life. **LIFE IS WHEN YOU HOLD THE DREAM IN YOUR THOUGHTS AND GET YOURSELF TO IT, THAT'S LIFE.** That process of getting to the dream, the BEST, when you make that decision.

So, as of right now this instant, forget your past, forget that you're ugly, forget that you're poor, forget that you're Dad disowned you, forget that you abused your power upon others, forget that you're being bullied, forget that you can't speak well or have no education, forget that you don't even know where your next paycheck is coming from, and do the following right NOW, right where you stand, this instant.

Say:-

(A.) I Forget The Past

I Have The Best Whitest Teeth
I Find The Best Foods To Eat That Are Great For My Body
I Have The Best Muscular Physique In The World

My Income Is Continuously Growing

I Receive A Lot Of Respect And I'm Paid Greatly

I Don't Work As Hard For The Basics

The Universe Gives Me All The Resources In Perfect Timing

I Give Love, Kindness, Care To Everyone I Come In Contact
With And Receive Lots Of Love Coming Back At Me Full Fold

I ___(The List Of What You're Going To Do)___
In Return For What I Desire From Life

My Competence Is At The Highest Level It Has Ever Been

Everyone Is Getting Me To My Destination

It Seems I Have An Exuberance Of Energy Every
Day I Awake To Do All Of My Tasks

Then:-

(B.) Listen To Yourself

Get back to your dreams, What were they? Look inside yourself, what is that one thing you do when no one else is looking? What do you want (to do or be)? How are you going to work with what you've been given?

Remember, what you want will never look like anything you've ever seen or done, feel like anything you've ever experienced or achieved. That's good. That's how you know you're on the right track. You're first remark is going to be, "How the hell am I going to do this!"

Remember what I said, life is not the everyday existence that you're living right now. You're supposed to decide on an impossible DREAM, hold the dream in your thoughts and get yourself to that DREAM with gusto, passion, desire, with everything you've got, and the universe can only but provide you with that which you've asked for.

Sketch Or Write What You Want Here

Sketch Or Write What You Want Here (continued)

(C.) Write Down A List

Make a list of what you're going to do in pursuit of your dream, your BEST, your highest goal. Write down a list of what you intend to do for what you desire from the universe. What are you going to do that will amount up to what you desire?

Remember, this is an exchange, it's the price you must pay for what you truly want, so if you want $600,000,000, you need to put a list together that will involve the things you need to do (with your MASTERMIND ALLIANCE group, don't forget them) that will produce that kind of riches. Start small, break it down, what can you do now? What can you do now with what you have? What can you do now with what you've been given?

Look at someone, a mentor, a celebrity, a college professor, a business owner, a senator, any visionary, someone who impresses you, someone you want to be like. What are they doing? Are you able to start something similar at your level? I looked at American actress, dancer, and singer Jennifer Lopez, net worth $400,000,000 in year 2023. She is always creating something, a new album, a new clothing line, a new perfume line, a new jewelry line, a new film, and the list goes on. Now your turn.

Hold the dream in your thoughts and you'll see, the universe will realize your dreams for you when you least expect them.

Sketch Or Write The List Of What You're Going To Do Here

Sketch Or Write The List Of What You're
Going To Do Here (continued)

(D.) Give And Make Yourself Better

American entrepreneur, author, and motivational speaker, Jim Rohn, in his book The Keys To Success, wrote, "We get paid for bringing value to the marketplace; The way that you become rich is by focusing on making yourself better".

Read the books to gain more understanding, learn a new language, learn a new software application, develop yourself, hone your craft, develop your competence and your creativity in what you do, put in the work, sell your dream to the public for the next 6 years nonstop, don't waste any time. This is the expression of the highest self, spiritual awakening, creating, developing, producing, gaining the value in yourself, improving your knowledge and skills, in pursuit of your dreams, in pursuit of being the BEST, in pursuit of your highest goal. This is what starts the attraction of wealth to you, and soon, the generation of profits.

Bringing value to the marketplace is producing, always producing, something for the public, creating, always creating, something that helps the public solve a problem, in a myriad of ways.

So, you should always be working on getting something out to the public, all the time, nonstop, always giving.

Sketch Or Write The First Twelve (12) Things
You're Going To Do With Your Riches Here

Sketch Or Write The First Twelve (12) Things You're
Going To Do With Your Riches Here (continued)

(E.) Receive And What You Save Must Earn, And Its Children Must Earn

Get ready to receive because it's sure to come. Budget your riches when they arrive, remember, your emergency fund, your retirement fund, your backup fund (my recommendation – 25% of the profits as protection), your business idea fund (for a research and development department or a mass marketing campaign). Setup wills to leave inheritances for the next generation, setup trusts to protect your assets from creditors and probates, setup power of attorneys who will make decisions for you when you're unable to do so in business and/or medical affairs. Then, ensure what you save from that wealth earn you profits, and those profits earn you more profits, according to your desire.

There are a lot of you who feel you're very poor at this time, and might be saying to yourself, "This is not for me, This is only for the elite rich". To you I say, start small, break it down, you will be rich too. For every dollar that you save, the proportion that goes towards your business idea, take those dollars and make them make you profits, then take a portion of those profits and make them make you more profits, according to your desire. Keep doing this for every dollar that you save and watch the change happen in your life too.

Now don't spend everything you make and then come back and say it doesn't work, No. For every dollar that you save, the proportion that goes towards your business idea, take those dollars and make them make you profits, then take a portion of those profits and make them make you more profits, according to your desire. Watch your riches grow every single year.

For the gig economy, you must sacrifice and set aside a portion of your check(s) for making profits, you have to. Some of your money must grow, must earn for you profits, and over time you too can enjoy financial independence.

For those in a full-time minimum wage circumstance, you have to sacrifice and set aside a portion of your wage(s) for making profits, you must. Buy and sell a product for profit, rent storage space for profit, try any multitude of ways to make profit, legally, of course.

In order to elevate yourself out of your circumstance, some of your money must grow, must earn for you profits, and over time you too will enjoy financial independence. Start where you are, at $0 if needs be, and work your way to the person you need to be.

A special note: There's always an offset for getting exactly what you want, though, and it's, also getting one thing you hate, one thing. I'll use American television host Steve Harvey's marriage as an example, if he doesn't mind, that is. He saw his wife to be, Marjorie, and instantly knew he would marry her. What comes with such a great wife is her home decoration style which can sometimes seem too much for Harvey. Harvey got exactly what he wanted, a great wife, but also got one thing about her that he may not like as much. Harvey's wife got exactly what she wanted, a great husband and provider, but also got one thing about him she may not like as much, his messiness. You will always get that in life. You cannot remove the thing you don't like as much, like her decoration style, and still have that particular great wife. You cannot remove his messiness, and still have that particular great husband, it doesn't work that way. The two go together, you have to work with her decoration style to enjoy that particular great wife. Or put another way, it's her particular large-scale decorative style that makes her the wife she is. That's just the Law of Duality.

So, same for you. When you finally get what you desire, there will be one little offset, there, that you too won't like. But not to worry, it comes with the package, you can't remove it though. It compliments and works well with your chosen desire.

Sketch Or Write The Twelve (12) Different Ways
You Are Earning Profits Right Now Here

Sketch Or Write The Twelve (12) Different Ways You
Are Earning Profits Right Now Here (continued)

Sketch Or Write The Twelve (12) Different Ways You
Are Earning Profits Right Now Here (continued)

(F.) Leave A Legacy

Sketch Or Write The Names Of The People In Your
Generation You Would Leave An Inheritance To Here

Sketch Or Write The Names Of The People In Your
Generation You Would Leave An Inheritance To Here

(continued)

"Assume the feeling of your wish fulfilled and Continue feeling that it is fulfilled until that which you feel objectifies itself."

– NEVILLE GODDARD, AUTHOR OF THE WISH FULFILLED

12 – KEEP CONNECTING TO UNIVERSE

For me, if you took everything away, knowing I died giving more than I received is all the contentment I desire.

When you give more love, more kindness, more care, they will come back to you full fold.

I implore churches to reveal the needed true information to their followers, really teach them, really inspire them, spiritually awaken them. We are at a time now where churches must do more, must improve, improve upon what has already been done, upon the needed change society craves, so, more value can be added to the global community.

Every one of us has this universal power. You could be in an impending automobile accident and command it not to happen today. That's the power you have. You could see a trailer truck about to accidentally run into a crowd of people, you can command it to stop. That's the power you have. That's the power everyone has. Your mind, what you believe you want to do, and the universe are amazing together (if done right).

When you're at your dream, doing your best, receiving your riches, keep connecting to universe, connecting to source, keep forgetting the past, keep listening to yourself for new directions, keep writing down a list, keep making yourself better, keep making your riches earn, keep leaving a legacy, and keep ensuring you give more love, more kindness, more care out into the world.

Note, it must be very clear in your psyche, how you would feel when you attain your dream. You cannot be in need and receive. You never find what you want, you find only that which you are. Author Neville Goddard, in his book The Wish Fulfilled, states "Assume the feeling of your wish fulfilled and continue feeling that it is fulfilled until that which you feel objectifies itself". Spend your days living your future days in your mind/your imagination/ your body, over and over again, feel exactly how you'd like to feel when you're at your dream, when you've attained your dream. According to Goddard, look as though you saw, listen as though you heard, stretch forth your imaginary hand as though you touched. The universe awaits what you feel is true and manifests it to you.

Here's another application of this principle. Let's say you see someone who irritates you very much. When you change your thought of how you see that person, for instance, by saying something to yourself like, "Paul is ideal as he is, Paul is getting me to my destination". The next time you see Paul you'll notice how he appears differently to you, he might even appear more helpful. You fulfilled the feeling you assumed. That's just the Law of Assumption.

Here's another. You're in a relationship. You go into it, for instance, by saying something to yourself like, "I love myself very much, I always take care of my every need, and I feel secure in who I am". You'll notice you receive love and care from your partner, in a secure environment because you had already imagined it for yourself, felt it for yourself to be already true.

Continue to keep connecting to universe, continue to assume the feeling of your wish, your dream, your desire fulfilled and continue feeling that it is fulfilled until that which you feel objectifies itself. Your new life now is, imagining the future you want, walking the walk, feeling the feelings, thinking the thoughts, to make it appear. That's living (done right).

BONUS: FOR PARENTS

I want this book to be in the hands of every individual who has a child, every individual who is thinking of having a child, everywhere in this world.

Firstly, as parents you already tell your kids to save their money at an early age. All of you have opened savings accounts for them to save from their weekly allowances and from their extra earnings.

What I want you to do now is step it up a notch. As parents, now tell your kids to earn on their saved money at an early age. All of you open Roth IRAs for your kids and guide them towards ventures that make a profit at an early age. Yes, the famous lemonade stand selling to their neighborhoods. Kids buy the raw materials with a portion of their saved money, sell lemonade, and earn a profit. Show them how to spend that profit. It's like I always say, 'Spend 30% (when you can), the remaining 70% – 10% to emergency like charities, 25% to retirement like Roth IRAs, 25% to backup, and the extra 10% to generate more profits.' Educate them as well on paying taxes, even as early as 3 years old. How you guide your kids will burn into their subconscious.

Secondly, now tell your kids to earn on their profits at an early age. Maybe, kids buy a new flavor with a portion of those profits, raise prices, and earn additional profits from that new flavor added. Show them again how to spend those additional profits. 'Spend 30%, the remaining 70% – 10% to emergency like charities, 25% to retirement like Roth IRAs, 25% to backup, and the extra 10% to generate even more profits.' And so on.

Thirdly, now let your kids see from an early age, that the reason they put away money is in exchange for things they may need in the future, so they don't have to work as hard. Open their eyes to the big life's purchases they may enjoy, when they make profits:-

-        Commercial real estates where they receive rental income and/or earn bigger profits

-        Existing businesses where they earn bigger profits

-        Stocks where they receive dividend income

-        Certificate of deposits where they receive interest income, even

-        Their first convertible and/or motorcycle, and/or

-        Their first computer and/or cellphone.

It is recommended that your kids know what net worth they'd like to have – the total value of all their assets less debts they'd like to have by the time they are age 30 – just like they know what they'd like to become when they grow up.

Other ventures that make a profit are:-

- Baked cookies delivery service
- Pet grooming services
- Garage sales
- Car washings
- Wedding photographs and videos
- Tutoring services
- Self-storage services
- Tools rental services
- Sell homemade games and toys
- Sell ice-cold water on summer hot days.

All kids, when they continue earning profits throughout life, will enjoy financial independence before age 30.

BONUS: FOR LGBTQIA + COMMUNITIES

I want to share with the LGBTQIA+ community a trick I learnt. This is geared towards the Lesbian Gay Bisexual Transgender Queer/Questioning Intersex Asexual (non-binary, pansexual, etc.) community and any person(s) or group(s) who feel they fall in this community.

Have you ever walked down the street, and say for instance, you saw a huge bulky strapping man walking towards you? Some of you may immediately feel threatened, and even move on to bulking up as well to protect yourself as you walk by him. Some of you may have already crossed the street to walk on the other side.

Now, let's say you saw a tiny man who looked like he couldn't hurt a fly, with no care in the world. A different reaction right? You would probably walk tall, but as per usual. Some of you might even go as far as ignoring him.

Why Do You Think This Is?

Ever notice when you meet someone you mirror who they present themselves to be? We tend to treat people the way they want to be treated, usually. That's why! And so, as soon as you saw those men approaching, you immediately mirrored their behavior.

Now LGBTQIA+ community and anyone who feels they're not accepted or don't fit in or just plain don't feel comfortable around people, use this mirroring trick:-

- First, accept yourself (the exact way you are, the way you think, the way you dress)
- Second, walk down the street like no one can change anything about you (speak the way you want to speak, live the way you want to live, legally, of course, dress the way you want to dress, train people in the way you want to be treated, what name should we call you?)
- Third, observe how people now treat you in return... It's exactly how you want to be treated.

With that said, no more suicides because you're gay. The world will see you and accept you when YOU have already done so yourself, meaning when you are very comfortable with YOU. The world is a mere reflection of how you see yourself (so if you see yourself as a lesbian who does not fit in, the world will treat you as a lesbian who does not fit in). Once you walk the way you want to walk, talk the way you want to talk, be the way you want to be, legally, of course, the world can only but treat you that exact same way.

And as quickly as is possible, start making more films that show the LGBTQIA+ community population already in receipt of acceptance and moving swiftly towards bigger and brighter hopes and dreams like – gold at the Olympics, #1 trillionaire on the Forbes list, President of the United States of America, world's greatest professional golfer, celebrating 50th year wedding anniversaries, and so on.

BONUS: FOR BUYING COMPANIES

A 3 year old should be buying companies, as well. Why not? I'm particularly focused on kids being rich early, getting to the point in their lives where they are functioning at their highest selves, getting there before age 30. Parents I call upon your active participation in this area; guide kids to earn profits earlier.

Buying existing companies provide fully trained human resources, established customer base, already defined operating expenses, existing supply chains, an inventory of goods, capital, assets, revenue, profits. So, get first-hand knowledge on how to do this early.

Firstly, you can either buy a company with debt (lend money to the company with the expectation of getting that money back) OR with equity (buy shares in the company with ultimately the majority shareholder owning the assets).

Secondly, once you've identified an existing company for sale (boring simple businesses like laundromats, rental properties, self-storage facilities, trucking companies, vending machine companies, senior care centers, car washes, according to business investor Codie Sanchez), then understand why that business is up for sale. Is its:-

- Competitors too far ahead?
- Business debts too high?
- Location a problem?
- Brand an issue?
- Owner near retirement?
- Sale on the market for several months with no buyers?

Ensure you evaluate the value of the business by examining its:-

- Tax returns audited by a certified public accountant
- Balance sheets, profit and loss statements, cash flow statements
- Sales records and accounts receivable
- Accounts payable
- Debt disclosures
- Advertising costs
- Property documents and equipment/asset listings including all vehicles
- Intellectual property assets
- Core processes

Thirdly, have a well-structured terms of sale to close and use seller financing (e.g. a portion of the profits of the company go towards repayment to the seller).

Fourthly, fix up the business and raise the prices.

Fifthly, offer more services to the customers.

Sixthly, buy the competitor, then repeat these six (6) steps.

Then, sell the company for 3-6 times more in 3-6 years.

ABOUT THE AUTHOR

Ready to be rich early?

How I Got To The Person I Needed To Be is the most useful modern-day personal financial-advice book that has influenced trillions of successful executives, entrepreneurs, and pioneers the world over.

MICHELE WILLIAMS, professionally known as *Williams*, is an American media and entertainment entrepreneur, author, motivational speaker, and philanthropist, who wrote the book to show you the money fundamentals to make you rich early.

He was born on Friday, December 14, 1973, in Andrews Memorial Hospital, St. Andrew, Jamaica. Mother, Thelma Elaine Lattibeaudierre, a working-class law-abiding typist, and father, Neville Adolphus Williams, a strong disciplinarian and hard-working insurance salesman. Williams, the eldest of three children, attended St. Augustine University in Trinidad where he completed a BSc in Computer Engineering. After been fascinated with computers and acted in much campus productions, Williams' artistic talent was born. Williams pursued an MBA in Corporate Finance at Manchester University, United Kingdom, and has been an advocate for kids being financially intelligent from an early age.

Williams' move to Los Angeles, California inspired his first film production Come Home to a Feminine Woman (2010) and first book How I Got To The Person I Needed To Be (2023). Williams has been pioneering media and entertainment, and advocating kids early financial intelligence ever since.

When you are ready to be rich, and ready to start using, very early, the money fundamentals you learn, this book is right for you.

www.ingramcontent.com/pod-product-compliance
Lightning Source LLC
Chambersburg PA
CBHW062345290526
45794CB00005B/2104